EVERYDAY LOVE

For my family

The following poems have been published:

Life After Death... *Eye on Life Magazine*
Photograph...*Talking Stick 22*
November 5, 1915...*Goose River Anthology*
How To Make Blueberry Pie...*Wilda Morris Poetry Challenge*
Ironing Skill....*Dust and Fire*
Lunch Guest, 1939...*Verse Wisconsin*
Pen Pal...*Wisconsin Poets Calendar*
Trilliums...*Rav'n*
Return Trip... *Wisconsin People and Ideas Magazine*
January Snow...*Talking Stick 21*
Bridge Club...*Verse Wisconsin*
Everyday Love...<u>*Golden Words*</u>
Surrender... *Wilda Morris Poetry Challenge*
Home Place...*Thunderbird Review*
my mother on steps....*Fifty Haikus*
picking blueberries.....*Wilda Morris Poetry Challenge*
snow early this year....*Haiku Journal*
giving it up...*Talking Stick*
Vigil...<u>*Verse and Vision, 2012*</u>

CONTENTS

Life After Death   1
Photograph   2
November 5, 1915   3
How To Make Blueberry Pie   4
Ironing Skill   5
Lunch Guest, 1939   6
Trilliums   7
Pen Pal   8
Return Trip   10
What's Due   11
Empathy   12
Home Again   13
January Snow   14
Something to Celebrate   15
Bridge Club   16
Everyday Love   17
Good Old Joe   18
Surrender   19
My Mother's Ring   20
Pa's Stir Fry   21
What Mother Planted   22
Upgrade   23
Home Place   24
Orchard   25
Haiku   26
giving it up   27
Vigil   28

Life After Death

My father never gets
the hang of being dead.
He lived so long, so willingly,
he never accepts his life
is finished, done, kaput.
He appears at family gatherings,
presence comforting as wood smoke,
laughter swirling through the stories.
On trips out of town,
he grumps in the back seat,
now that he can't call shotgun.
This afternoon, there he was
at the table by the window,
easing his back into the sun,
looking for a cup of coffee
and a cinnamon roll.

Photograph

Posed in the yard
Sophie, sitting, holding baby Ellen
husband Victor standing
wearing his suit jacket and good hat
hand on Wayne's shoulder.

My father, age four,
shirt buttoned to the neck
hair slicked, pants safety pinned
hiding a bit behind his mother's arm.
He looks intently into the camera lens
to what's coming.
Past losing his right eye when he is ten
past the 1918 Hinckley fire
that takes their house and cows
and burns his pet ram black,
into that most terrible part
when his dad dies
leaving all eight of them and Sophie
on the farm with no aid or money.
He is already sad.

He can't see just a little farther.
Far enough to see me
standing on the porch, waving.

November 5, 1915

Cooling herself after baking bread
on the wood stove late at night,
my grandmother was
found dead on the stoop.
Mother was nine.

Days before,
walking together on the short cut.
Grandmother stopped
to make a cairn of rocks.
"A memorial," she said.

Children on the homestead
were expected to be strong,
to understand death
is a necessary part of living.

I asked Mother once
if she had been very sad,
lost and lonely.
She said "No,"
she was cared for,
being the last of eight.
Life on the farm went on.

All her long life,
she felt for little beings:
helpless people, hurt animals.

And she collected rocks,
which, easily found,
last forever.

How to Make Blueberry Pie

Enter Quinton swamp at last year's faded marker.
Keep up with Pa, in his eighties and leading.
Deep in woods, where berries hang like grapes,
powdery blue, warm, kneel.

Listen. "When I was six we took the horses….
water got warm and butter melted on the bread…."
Pretend you never heard of the 1918 fire.
"Dad put us eight kids in a circle in the field….
My pet ram was killed because he was burned black…"

When your pail is full, blindly follow Pa
through brush slapping your face. Have faith.
You come out right in front of the truck.
Admire the pickings. "By God, we did pretty good."

Clean berries at picnic table under the pines.
Make crust while Pa makes filling.
Talk about how great berries were last year,
or was it the year before? "Man, it was just blue…."

Let Pa slice it. "Gramma Uitto cut hers in four…."
Put ice cream on your piece to cool it,
use a spoon for juice. Smack your lips and laugh
when Pa scrapes his plate, says again, "That'll sell!"

Ironing Skill

When I was trusted to iron
my father's shirts,
white, starchy, cotton,
I took my time.
Smoothing the yoke,
then the sleeves, both sides,
the cuffs, inside and out,
then the shirt front, and back,
and around to the other side.
At the last, the collar, taking care
there were no creases by the points.
I hung them on hangers in the closet,
with all the buttons facing right.
At breakfast, I sat proudly as he ate,
ready for work, looking good,
no wrinkles in the collar.

Lunch Guest, 1939

Mom, who's that man on the steps?
    Just somebody passing through.
Why is he here?
    Because he was hungry.
What is he eating?
    A fried egg sandwich.
And coffee?
    Yes, and coffee.
Why is he eating out there?
    He said he liked it outdoors.
How did he know where we lived?
    I guess they tell each other.
Where is he going?
    Back to the train, I think.
Is he ever coming back?
    Probably not.
Why did he call you "Ma'am"?
    I think he was just being polite.

Trilliums

When snow melts
in the deepest shadows
of our Wisconsin woods,
white of wild trilliums
takes its place.
Though my father understood
the state has claimed them
as their own
and threatens fines
for anyone who argues,
he dared every May
to walk the south forty,
surprising
his sweetheart
with a large bouquet
of spring
offered in his wide
calloused hand.

Pen Pal

The Evening Telegram printed
names of soldiers wanting mail.
Mother chose Robert Smith.
Wrote, in teacher's Palmer script,
of ordinary happenings
in our little Wisconsin town.
What birds were at the feeder,
the fox or deer she saw,
how much snow fell,
hoping he was doing well.
Nothing sad or troublesome.
She wrote often, all during the war.

Sometimes, a letter thanking her
would come from a distant battle place,
Italy, or France maybe,
with the military post mark.
A.P.O. 45, New York,
censored by army examiner.

War ended in August, '45.
The following Christmas,
a card arrived
showing a black man
sitting by the decorated tree.
He was afraid, if she knew,
letters "from home" would stop.

It made no difference, she confided.
He was fighting for us all,
and she was his pal.
For more than fifty years,
his greeting was saved in her shoebox

with anniversary cards from Pa,
and fancy old valentines.

They didn't write much longer.
He was back home then,
and that war was over.

Return Trip

Coming back always went fast.
We fell asleep on the rear seat
in happy tangle, and were home
before we wished it.
My father carried us
to our beds, my younger
brothers limp and soft,
easily moved.
I was too old
for such attention,
and feigning sleep
I'm sure he knew.
He picked me up,
all dangling legs and arms,
my face in his shoulder
of tobacco and wool,
trudged up the stairs.
By hall light,
he put me down gently,
took off my shoes,
covered me up, clothes and all.
Then, tip toed out,
leaving the door ajar.

What's Due

Pa switched me once.
Don't remember what for.
Made quite a show of it, though.
Went out in snow
for a willow branch.
Laid it on top of the heater
to thaw so it had a little spring.
Gave me a minute to rue my deed,
then, a couple stinging whacks
on the backs of my skinny legs.
Like I said, don't remember what for.
It never became a habit.

Empathy

Warren Nelson dumped me
for a sophomore
with curly hair and straight teeth.
I was numbed.
Secured in a blanket
of self pity
on our green friese sofa
I pretended to read.
My brothers ignored me,
the family went to bed.
The house grew chilly.
I stared
at History of the United States.

When the clock chimed
twelve
on the kitchen shelf
my mother
in her nightgown
peered around the corner
pretending to check
the thermostat.

She dispensed her usual
prescription:
"Just go to bed now.
It will be better
in the morning."

Sometimes, it was.

Home Again

Home is where
they have to let you in
when you go there,
my dad would say,
misquoting Frost.
I left too soon,
confident, sure,
needing no help.
I came back
with a toddler
and a newborn,
humiliated
by poor choices,
without energy
or direction.
I kept my eyes
on the familiar hall tile.
My mother took
the wailing baby.
My father said,
"Sit down,
and eat."

January Snow

The snow floats
like feather confetti,
two feet of down
rounding all edges
to softness.

Not like snow
my father remembered
when Dakota wind
ruthlessly blew blizzard across
Minnesota for days,
blinding everything white.
Cattle were lost,
tracks covered in seconds.
Grandfather strung a rope
from house to barn
so boys doing chores
could find their way back.
People died in that snow.

This snow stills breath
with grace,
thrills mind with wonder.
Pristine beauty,
welcome as praise.

Something to Celebrate

When he was still in college
John and Darlene eloped.
Crossed over state line into Minnesota
one day without warning.
When Pa came home
from his construction job,
found us all sitting in the living room
with the news,
he went to wash up.

Twenty minutes later
he came out, cleanly shaven,
in a white shirt and tie
wearing his best suit.
Dressed for the occasion
he strode across the room
to offer congratulations,
to shake my brother's hand,
man to man.

Bridge Club

During the big war,
women in our village
formed a bridge club,
there being no formal entertainment,
unless you count Ladies Aid
or the Co-op Guild,
and the school Christmas program
at the town hall.

They took turns being hostess
and everyone dressed to "go out."
Did their hair in pincurls and curlers,
put on their best dresses, earrings,
their good silk stockings,
taking care to get the seams straight.
Wore their high heels, applied lipstick.
Sprayed perfume, did their nails.

Two tables were set up,
the house slicked spick and span.
Lunch served after cards was fancy,
even with rationing.
Shrimp salad, maybe,
the toast cut in triangles,
or chicken ala king in tiny pastry puffs.
Desserts were edible art,
frosted tarts, maraschino cherries,
real whipped cream.

Every other Monday night
we kids watched amazed
as our ordinary mothers
transformed themselves into ladies
for bridge club.

Everyday Love

Even in his eighties
my father leaped into each day
with such enthusiasm
he never stopped to consider
why his life seemed to go
so smoothly.

His cap was on the hall shelf
when he reached for it
instead of on the t.v.
where he left it,
car keys handy
right next to the phone.
His pea soup never burned,
though he wandered into
the living room
telling his story.
The towel he put on the mantle
was back on the rack.
Whole wheat bread was
baked in round loaves
to give him four heels,
his pillow was fluffed
on his night call to the bathroom.
and he was discretely reminded
not to swear
when we had company.

My mother had his back.
Between them,
they had it all under control.

Good Old Joe

Pa bought Joe thinking
he was a pure bred Black Lab.
Soon it became clear there
had been a scandal in the family.
His hair grew long and curly,
his build stocky.
He was a quiet dog,
patient, intelligent, responsive.
Always ready to go exploring,
waiting at the mailbox
for the school bus.
Over the years his fear
of loud noise grew--
guns and thunderstorms
caused him to quiver
and come into the house,
once ripping our screen door
to shreds in his panic.

In old age he got distemper
with no cure known.
Pa took his gun and called,
twice because the gun
was obvious, and walked
with him to the far edge
of the field, by the woods.
The first shot missed
as tears blurred Pa's vision.
Joe sat still and waited
for the second.

Surrender

After ninety-three years,
we reversed roles.
Remember? You were brought
to the table and sat waiting.
It was right before you gave up
eating all together,
putting your arm across your mouth
to make the point.
You were agreeable,
smiling and patient.
I was the one mashing the food
and feeding you cheerfully,
coaxing you to take
just one more bite.
I had assumed that I would do
the works you didn't have time
to finish….sorting your photos,
publishing your journal,
doling out your treasures.

In a flash, I realized you were also
giving me Pa,
though we had competed
for his attention
almost seventy years.
The look on your face
I had waited for all my life,
that trust, and adoration.

My Mother's Ring

Had orange blossoms
carved in the white gold band
when it was new.
Her finger grew around it
like a tree around a string of wire.
Her knuckle aged bigger than the ring,
the orange blossoms all wore off.

When she died,
the director handed me
her boxed ashes
and a plain white envelope.

They should have asked me first.
I would have said, "No.
Leave it."
so, wherever she went,
they would know she belonged
to Pa.

Pa's Stir-Fry

When Pa was ninety-three
he invited us for shrimp stir-fry.
The platter was heaped with
precision cut vegetables.
"Pa," I said, "That's beautiful!
Where's the shrimp?"

"DAMMIT!" he bellowed,
"Tell you what. You come back
tomorrow night and I will
remember the shrimp!"

Sure enough.
The next night, the platter
was heaped with precision cut
vegetables and lots and lots
of plump pink shrimp.

"Wow, that's beautiful, Pa," I said.
"Pass the rice."

"DAMMIT!" he bellowed.

What Mother Planted

Daffodils
still surprise us,
popping up here and there
like hope
at the edge of the wild yard.
Iris make a quiet show,
huddling
in their little group.
Pink and white phlox
bloom every summer
along the old rail fence,
and the oak,
grown from an acorn
picked during a visit to her birthplace
in her seventies,
now would tower over her house,
if her house was still there.

Upgrade

In his eighties,
Pa took the saw
to one of his best
wooden spoons.
Made the end flat
to better cover the bottom
of the pan
when he made rice pudding.
I have it now.
It lends a little flavor
to everything I stir.

Home Place

After Pa died
no one wanted to sleep
in the house
across the field
where for so many years
we gathered gleefully.
Now just an empty box,
even his dog felt lost,
sitting on the porch
though we offered treats
to come in.

We all chose reminders
of his ninety-eight years:
coffee cups, books,
fishing rods, tackle, guns.
Donated the rest to charity.

We scattered the ashes,
kept the land with his spirit,
sold the house to be moved
and did not look back
when they lifted it on a trailer
and drove away.

Orchard

Ma and Pa's ashes
rest under the wide spruce
on the way to the orchard,
shielded by a common field stone,
names on a small brass plaque.
I greet them as I hurry by.

Though my father did not believe
in life after death,
he materializes quickly.
Today, when invited,
they join me
as easy as sunlight.

"Oh," I hear my mother sigh,
white hair blending with blossoms.
My father slows by the plum,
saying, "You could prune this branch."

We linger,
marveling at cherry flower,
high bush cranberries,
exploding clouds of pale bloom.

I leave them circled in Spring.
She, snapping a small sprig to smell,
he, watching her, smiling.

Haiku

my mother on steps
watching for bluebird she hears
calls me to come, sit

picking blueberries
in Pa's favorite patch
gone now seven years

snow early this year
today I cut Father's shirts
into quilt patch squares

giving it up

cows
raising chickens
gardening big time
canning tomatoes
traveling abroad
fishing in Alaska
feeding birds in winter
canoeing upstream to fish
walking four miles a day
cross country skiing
flying across country by himself
deer hunting
wife of sixty-nine years
cooking for company
computer correspondence
golf
exercises on the floor
picking raspberries
lifting weights in a chair
driving
baking bread
walking
making it to a hundred
asking to come home
everything

Vigil

I held my father's hands
while he died.
Extra-large-glove-sized hands.
By the thumb, wide faded reminder
of the axe at seventeen.
Crooked finger, broken by the mower.
Myriad silver scars.
Calluses softened now.
Fingers that routinely hit
two computer keys,
drummed the table when impatient,
or bored.
Knuckles aged bony, veins dark and visible.
At ninety-eight, the vellum skin
blotched.
Hands that skinned deer, built houses,
crimped pie crust.

We waited,
his firm grasp warm in mine.
When a thousand stars exploded,
he squinted hard,
and let me go.

Made in the USA
San Bernardino, CA
09 January 2015